Unashamed

Unashamed

REVEALING TRUTH

BY

Melanie Joyce Johnson

www.bookstandpublishing.com

Published by
Bookstand Publishing
Morgan Hill, CA 95037
Record 4180_2

ISBN 978-1-61863-935-6

In memory of,
my sweet grandmother Martha
You are a missing portion of joy in my soul

CONTENTS

Revealing Truth

Unashamed is a series of poems about exposing the vulnerable space between truth and reality. It is an unlocking of the inexpressible joy that satan has sealed. It is a revealing of themes that materialize in the lives of women: the wounds, the worship, the (un) forgiveness [of self, others, parents, culture], the search for identity [and who and what has to be left behind in order to *find* it], the candidness of corruption in the church, and the aftereffects of embracing negative strongholds. *Unashamed* is a spiritual revelation of a human condition.

Melanie's premiere collection of poetry began with a desire to articulate and reveal *her* truth by uncovering the shame of *her* hidden scars. She expresses in **I Have a Right**:

> *"From twenty-three to thirty I gave it up, gave one away, lost a lot,*
> *but gained me."*

Melanie extracts the lies we conceal by spoon-feeding us with a sweet dose of truth in **Five-Finger Discount**:

> *"glutinous hands confiscate and complicate simplicity*
> *as gluttony devours the unripened fruit of our hood."*

Melanie discloses how to forsake the spaces that have hurt us in the past which keep us from reaching our full potential of intimate worship with the Lord. She voices in **Fall for Him**:

> *"Falling Unashamed, I lay*
> *There, prostrate before Him*
> *Wound up my wounds in*
> *Willing worship and*
> *Waited while He welcomed my*

Her easy to read poems are fitted to remind us to search for that which will set us free and help us to become unashamed to reveal truth.

Part 1: Girl

Limited Edition

Thug eyes
Entice
Virgin
Minds
Release
Fresh fruit
From
Fertile
Vines
49¢ a pound
come one
come all
come eat
While
Supplies last

Five-Finger Discount

untried her ambiance
behind the ears aqueous
naiveté sitting there between mama's legs
bathing in a sea of jeweled cornrows
her sole existence lies in popsicle dreams while
candy-coated nightmares yield sugary screams
and melt in hushed lullabies
warm milk and vanilla permit pubescence easy rest
here now no sign of empty in mama's nest
but she our burgeoning sugar and spice has
breathed everything nice except reality
she was smooth and subdued 'til she
laid eyes on a fool
then aged insecurity snatched the woman
out of baby girl and forced her to
grow up too soon
glutinous hands confiscate and complicate simplicity
as gluttony devours the unripened fruit of our hood
now Ms. Thang at 16
taking down them cornrows
proclaiming in ebonic conundrums the frivolous
intellect of callow lovers
supine she lay between silk sheets, musty flesh,
and old spice—stripped of virgin fidelity
her furtive gems exposed
barren by lecherous rhapsody
baby girl and philanderer unite in an
unrequited acquiescence
of love

Scent of the Bushes

the aroma of wild sunflowers merge
with the natural scent of the bushes
mild yet pure blossoms detonate
nonstop
ecstatic morning sensations
beckon him into the harem of my love
here erotic dreams originate
and Nubian doves nest
rest my spiritual side
as satanic-angelic
wings take flight   basking in the
memory of this glorious immoral night
the smell of Shea butter and strawberries unite
with the natural scent of the bushes
pure blossoms explode perpetually
leaving the ground quaking   awaiting
the moonlit rhapsody of love
we drink everlastingly until merry
and place our spiritual minds outside the realm
of our intimate crime of passion

Fingerprints on God's Temple

got 10 sets of fingerprints on God's temple/God's temple
20 hands polishing my curves
100 fingers waxing my behind
10 sets of fingerprints on God's temple/this temple/God's
temple/His temple/God's temple/this temple
ashamed but not insane
ashamed that my claim to fame won't be
Academy Award Winner
for
Best Lead Actress
who waited 'til marriage
go
and sin no more in this temple/His temple
100 fingers sweeping my kitchens
shampooing my carpets
God's temple/God's temple/God's temple
is dirty needs cleaning
this temple/God's house
this vessel is God's temple
I need a shower or two or ten douches
in God's temple/God's temple
God's temple
Holy Spirit drowning in His temple/His temple
someone throw Him a latex lifesaver, a Trojan will do
10 sets of fingerprints on God's temple
20 hands buffing God's temple
100 fingers waxing my behind
in God's temple/His temple/God's temple/this temple

Part 2: Home

The Porch

I stand in the middle of my floor, in 11-year-old frame
mosey to the edge of my twin bed gripping my Lisa Frank
Trapper Keeper
and dolphin pin
I jot one word...touchable then
memory now
ABUSE
I knew it well
too well
oh well
too familiar with it to dare forget it
I'm hurting, but
she's bleeding,
laughing at me for loving so hard
I cringe at her yelp
I smell smoke
Virginia Slims and Newports
whites of my eyes now red
from broken love
I escape to the porch
not afraid
just   away
from
that
word
before it becomes physical again

Home

The family ties are
severed
no one knows how to love anymore
what to even love for
it's a shame
The family
divided itself by adding secrets to its fragile lifelines
negativity is a daily delicacy
and pity opens the morning shades
crazy love is this family curse
generational ignorance rebirths   itself
would rather be adopted in
or married in
to not have the bloodline of absurdity, insolence,
inherited.
where has family gone
why haven't we grown to learn to lean
on each other
instead we hold greed and
be in emotional need for
psychological schemes against each other
Family is not a game
it's the name that God placed
on His elect
but we sling mud and trample on
or forget where we came from
Home.
where the heart is   broken
Home.
where innocence is   stolen
Home.

has lost its place in the human race
Home is the new black [sheep] abode
yet no one wants to go
back there anymore…too many lies
so many cries.
the crimes increase and we never achieve a thing.
The family ties are
severed
constantly creating negative cycles with the training wheels
left on

Giving Flowers (*read in memory of Martha Roberson, March 1, 2013*)

I walk easy in her diamond-laced footprints
She left them for me
My birth-stoned April baby
Turned woman of God
Free from her pain
And suffering no more named
Among her
My super-addendum-mama
My grandmother doesn't have to hurt for me no more
Doesn't have to pray
For me.
No more want for her
only worship
No more pills for her
only praise
Please stay with me grandma my heart sings
We selfishly
want her home, but she worshipfully beckons us from there
To lay our burdens down
here
Because now her soul sees
that yes… God is Real
He's Real
For her soul rests full well in His bosom
I'm like her in my own unique way
Like the way she used to exclaim,
Melanie, don't you want to make US some popcorn?
Of course I do, just like you taught me
Just like you fought for me to have what I needed in my
preteen years

Like showing up to my best friend's birthday party with
rollers in your hair...
To teach me a lesson on
Respecting my elders, when you told me, "you can't stay long,
so come on out when I get there..." yes ma'am...
I still remember that day,
Ashamed, but
You
You were so cleverly
Teaching and molding me spiritually
And though I knew it
You made sure I proved it
by being baptized
Now as I teach women how
To be like you
Because you were like Christ
I smile,
knowing my 30 years with you were so worthwhile
So I close here to say
She'd want me to tell you that
Yes, God is real
He's So Real in my soul
Because I know
He's taken her from a place of pain
A place of turmoil
and
Sealed her in Spirit
Healed all of her trials
And wrapped her in
Sweet Joy
She is Filled
no longer with fear
She toils no more here

But cheers
Forever
She has no more
Regrets
The woman of God in my life
Is now waiting
Expectantly for us
to Get Right Church and Let's Go Home
Waiting
For me
For us
As we follow
in her diamond-laced footprints
Because
She is now free

Remember September

Crimson leaflets crumbled into eyes
Like cigarette ashes burning holes
The cool walk with a brisk swag
Skipping like pimps primping for a fix
Aggravation sells like a hooker on the
Corner
Disguised in fishnets and pumps
Remember September smells of day old
Jimmy Dean sausage and chilidogs
      most of all memories flood reality
      most of all tears make soft welcome mats
      most of all September is unforgettable
      most of all heartaches happen in the fall
Not only does weather turn cold, but
Hearts turn sometimes too
Turn cold
Watch your emotions next September
Remember
      who taught you that all sums don't add up
Remember
      when innocence was taken and not offered
Remember
      where dreams only made sense to the drunken fool
Remember
      how words used to slice smoother than Ginsu knives
Remember
      what you learned about love yet forgot to exercise
Remember
September
You may wanna wrap up before going outside next time

Part 3: Transformation

Uncomfortable Transitions

an unreachable itch
ignored
its flagrant beckoning
an annoying twitch
transitional words beg change
growth
movement
foul play to transform from the comfort
of norm
to reigning sin I bid obeisance
bringing noise to deafen the Spirit within
movement getting over self
tripping over familiarity
changing character into Christ-mind
His now mine as I cross
streets, clutching contempt's soft hand
New Self's constant renewal an
unwelcoming chore
harassing scutwork
I surrender to virtue because I'm defined
by divine circumstance
dutiful demands displaced and
mistraced steps of a master
slick as a robber's key
a wise thief lives in me
code switching in the blink of cataractic eyes
successful change a neoteric, uncharted tribulation
uncomfortable transition crosses over to love
trust its new name
losing one's mind and
loosing straight jackets of time

a new budding masterpiece perceived, but never plucked
acting my Christian age
like a
new babe
leaping face first in damnable ditches
happily fluffing my twiggy pillows
yet afraid
of change
loving the sensation of an unreachable itch
influencing others in my refusal to scratch

Block

In the flesh
a warm caress
opens me
My emotions capsized
I reminisce
of sure times when
rhymes made sense
Leaking linguistics in a cinch
Refresh my memory
wasn't love a trip
Each moment on the
brink of a tiptoe
Slow
then harvest
Vacant images in vindictive
fields of woe
Morning brings mental light
when pen refuse to write
Then I compose prose in shape,
Form,
Color,
Rhythm
Speaking in apostolic gisms
Dancing in mountainous metaphors
Strolling in simplistic similes shores
Loathing the lethargic language
of broken speech
I
  T
   U
   M

  B
    L
      E
from the heights I reach
as my words spill forward—BREECHED
Revealing truth feet first and
Bearing new life to my reticent reflections
of
free
verse

The Hold Up

Nullified nouns, vicarious verbs
      Rejected
Symmetrical similes and mellifluous
      Metaphoric schisms on love   lost,
                                                gained

      Heartaches and breaks
      Wills made
      Goals forged and   forgotten
Gargantuan past participles and
Cosmic prepositional phrases which
Compose who me is, have sucked themselves
into a black hole of   silence, an oblivious new
                            shame
Am I afraid?
Pen strokes become vacant memories to times when they
flowed ceaselessly
conveying my joys
but more fluently   my woes
I have fallen to a swift demise
I   laugh at my struggles
      shrug off my thoughts
      stifle my soul words instead of   release them
I   sleepwalk into stations of   mental blocks
Where true life's work
Is   castrated
        procrastinated
        underestimated
Reclaim consciousness of identity before legacy breeds an
                      anonymous shadow
Forever vanished

Confetti

Mixed up   cut up   crumbled up   confusion
        falls to
earth   to cover the   groves of   refuted dreamers
fantasies fates' twisted
'cause they   missed it   when it was told
        them   to
                            regroup
like   raspberry   raindrops cooling the   grapy
haze   of
                          morning's   citrus dew
The breeze delights you with   the fall of   sweet
honeycomb
leaves   dropping
        onto your face
        Open mouth   to   catch the   great sensations
        flow in
           directions
           unknown
In   pieces it   descends   to the earth   to splash
      your   dented
      demeanor to utter   extravagance   happiness
      rains   down
from   the   boundless
     sky   to
        wanting   lovers
        hands
Hatred   fading   love cascading   like serene
        waterfalls
beneath the   cliffs down to   the river
    bottoms'   edge dripping
    haphazardly
does   it   fill up   fields of   war

                to   bring   peace
rain   down
            glory
            from   our Father   Oh, how the
            blessings
                              plunge
to   give us   all   peace   of mind   to
            find   the   right
            one   this
                              time

Don't Stop

Getting lost in the coast
Mind adrift to a steady limit of speeding
thoughts
Not ready to stop at the red light
of awareness
In tuned to blotchy static-ky stations
I'm coming to, to myself
Committed to past reflections and future's
unknown directions.
Swerving around curves and
crashing because the beat won't stop
I mean police won't drop
the charges
against racing thoughts
I get lost in the coast
the enjoyment of nothingness is silenced
Pavement crushed
As I pay the price for ignoring
the fuss
of truth
In my rear view

Cat in the Rain

I am the cat who liked the rain
I threaten gravity
I never obey
        I sleep in a purple crush velvet basket
I'm tired of chasing the yarn and blind mice indoors, so
I'm stepping out
You finish my chores
        I'm exceeding all the expectations
Breaking all the rules before they're set
I'm a cat dancing in the rain
A black cat at that
        I dare you to curse my mane
I'm not bound to catnip and cat naps
I'll snap and rig the mousetraps
I'm stepping on all the sidewalk cracks
      I'm a stray black cat dancing and singing in the rain
I dare you to cross me
I dare you to top me
I dare you to stop me
        You can't
I sleep when I want to sleep
Eat when you tell me not to eat
Independent and free to ignore you and be me
        I'm a cat.
I smell like flowers and walk on rainbows

Part 4: Soul

Swallowed Clause

Words hurt like steel pounding fragile bones
I'd rather chisel out some sticks and stones
To learn a lesson
God's not ready to teach
Spitting imitation texts and
Prosaic speech
Betting me to believe a lie
I've already made real
Saving grace passed by,
Removes all my general skill
Uneducated theory
Reigning intimate thoughts
Running behind time in
Hypothesized sweatshops
Verbally beaten for the clause I should
Have swallowed

The White Windmill

I witnessed them spinning and
turning around me
An out of control hurricane wind
I shivered
though marvelous the sight before me
White and magnificently
unimaginably an image
untouched by my hands
it turns my sin-sickness into
an ethereal eyesore
I run and jump on the blades
to catch my sins before they're
kinetically cleansed
for that is my only comfort
My soul going through the
empty nest syndrome
Who finds comfort in depravity?
I do.
The wind keeps blowing
the mill still going back and
forthcoming recharging my iniquities
My plight a
hollow vessel awaiting the Master's
use
A risky choice He makes
but does
Knowing I love hurricane season
A ubiquitous rush back to my
peaceful peccancy
Insatiably energized

Forgiving Me

I'm feeling weird
Like I don't belong here
Like a clown at a funeral
But this is not a joke

I'm feeling trapped
Like I'm out of place
Like a stray cat in a rainstorm
Who doesn't like getting wet

I'm feeling blue
Like an ink stain on white slacks
Like a deep motionless ocean
Like the saddest day of my life

I'm immersed in love's triangle
Emotionally acute
Proverbially obtuse
The four sides of my perimeter ache
This is not adding up

I'm feeling ashamed
Like I'm butt naked in a Broadway show
Like I've willingly given the stalker my address
Like I've brought this on myself

It's time for me to forgive me and move on.

Gold Tooth

God has a gold tooth
One smile stirs
Jealousy in the stars
The moon tries to outdo
But can't
A lunar loss
To the solar smile of morning

God has a gold tooth
Lights up my inhibitions
Exposes my insecurities
Emblazing my worth like a sharp shooter
Hitting his mark
I'm at a loss, but not lost
His brilliance covers me
O wake up my soul

God has a gold tooth
One smile stirs
Jealousy in the stars
The moon tries to outdo
But can't
A lunar loss
To the solar smile of morning

O wake up my soul

Part 5: Woman

Unreal

My feelings are unreal
Like a voodoo doll on wheels
Yet you
Poke and prod
and
Push and shove
until I fall over
I've had enough

He say   I do
She say   I move
Adjacent to their words
A stumbling groove

But, who do, voodoo best?
I do
A cotton-filled free woman
with one foot
And wooden legs

Wine Song

If I were a wine song
I would be a sweet fermented harmony of operatic lush notes
and apricot arias
A vintage love song
I would be a slow jazz dessert wine with a splash of honey
and blues, dripping half
Notes and flat vanilla tones from my lips that sparkle like
smooth champagne
If I were a wine song I would be
Dipping my hips in white grape scents and
Splitting perfect fourths off beat on purpose
Syncopating peachy rhythms with every sip
I would be a pomegranate spiritual
Baptizing minds with
My funkadelic stride if I were a wine song
I would be old school nectar, scatting mellow oranges in
syrupy flukes
My fingertips would tap dance with a citrus apple zest
I would be a never-ending symphony
Of classical rose blossoms
A rustic *Castello del Poggio*
I would be a saccharine finale to any meal

Tippy Toes

Surrounded by yesterday's snowflakes
A chestnut colored pool
Replaces
Crisp, white plumy streamers
Molded into snow angels
Today means tears wiped away
Grown woman standing on
Tippy toes to find herself
Sharing deep secrets with lovers
Like lassies at recess
Bursting through cocoon mesh
One stomp at a time only to
Emerge a one-winged violet
Butterfly, prayerfully wanton and coquettishly
Apologizing for unraveling so soon
Now fallen in lust
With dust in her lacy pants
Looking for the first participants
In her precarious rain flight of chance
Butterfly's heart broken and soiled
Wing spread overhead in defiant
Pursuit
Of her womanly figure
And purposed mister
Spiraling head first towards another snowflake stream
Rejected again
Yet feeling redeemed

Unashamed Blues

Picture. A girl spinning with the wind
Hula-hoop focus furrows her brow
Gyrating game creates a neighborhood spectacle
Ms. Willie Mae watches from her window   like always
Ms. Faye asks for a dollar then slips away like the one who
slipped a mickey in her drink
Mr. Earl scoots past with crumpled cigarette in hand blowing
O's as wide as the arc in her hips
whoosh. fun. smirk. twist.
Wrists high and taut as if she's placing coats over her forearms
to check them
Check. Her. Out.
She laughs, knowing this spiraling childhood sport of skill
makes grown men swallow deep and look away
She flirts like a mac daddy
Spinning and corkscrewing in her skirt
Mothers tell their sons, "playtime is over, supper's getting
cold, so get home"
Cross-legged female watchers
mimic her moves in their minds to use later
on baby-powder-dusted-flowered sheets with Mr. Right
        Now
She whirls   into the night
their staring faces disappear from the block
The moon illuminates this private dancer
Exposing the stamina in her well muscled calves
Tight tummy
Sweat puddles like a bubble bath in her clavicle
Sprinter's ecstasy slips down her thighs,
Arabesque loops   dent the earth
Sweet success anchors her ankles
Looking up into the purplish, orangey heavens

Unmoved in her groove
Unashamed of her blues
She bows to
Her body
Her ability
Her watchers
whoosh. fun. smirk. twist.
Her reasons for being alive   finally revealed.

SPOKEN WORD PIECES

Part 6: Master

Deliver

I'm about to deliver
Give birth to a mystery
Lay supine and extract a divine history in swaddling clothes
Pushing...
The crown of the Anointed One
Peeks out
We scream in unison
My Savior
Triumphs head first
Who is to be the head of my household; whether
Married
Single
Divorced
Widowed
The Head leads me
Pushing through the veiny thickness of my sin
I'm born again…
But He's the One living in me
Growing in me
Pregnant with expectant Jubilee
I'm about to deliver
Give birth to the only Begotten Son
My own child-Master
Nursing the Messiah as if He was
Born from my own womb
Yet, I'm the one sipping on the sincere milk of the Word
Wiping my mouth that tastes of the gospel
Pure, unadulterated, satisfying
Nutrition called fruit of the Spirit
I spit
Rhymes and seeds of

Love, Joy, Peace, Longsuffering, Gentleness, Goodness, Faith,
Meekness, Temperance
From which grows a garden that reminds me of Gethsemane
Where I fall to my knees
Bended and broken
Pleading take this cup away from me
I weep so hard
Tears fall like drops of blood because of
The labor that is before me
The Lord's work is too much for me to handle
I can't honestly share the scandal of deceit
Cheat the world with obedience to the Supreme
I'm ashamed that He's filled me
Afraid that I'll start showing
And then they'll start asking about what's growing in me
They wouldn't believe me if I said
Jesus is who's got me
Throwing up wickedness and
Glowing with a secret love that makes my eyes twinkle
And my soul sizzle
With the Holy Ghost leaping in me
I should keep this pregnancy to myself
Spiritual stoutness
Confused with legalistic devoutness
I'm hungering and thirsty for righteousness
Not craving ice cream and pickles
I'm craving the oracles of God
And the mystery of the deep things of the Lord in my temple
That no one knows but the Spirit
I'm about to deliver
Him who was delivered for my offenses
Raise Him who was raised for my innocence
I'm about to give birth to my very own
Blessed Redeemer

I should be the Arrested
Re-Schemer
Because I can't seem to let Him loose from my tubes
satan has me all tied and twisted got me all confused
Thinking I'll give birth to a stillborn fool
Never! The less
I'm about to deliver a miracle
Who knew me before my existence
I'll faithfully pull Him out of my womb
A tomb that wants to keep Him buried and hushed
And watch how He will make me to grow in wisdom and in
stature and in
favor with
God and man
Oh man
This faith gives me access to grace
I dare not blaspheme my child of God to His face
I have an intense love jones
For the One who did no wrong
Him, who was hung on the cross
Suspended in my spirit
Who cohabitates with me
It's a rebirth
Because He is
The firstborn from the dead sin in me;
Appointed heir of all things
Anointed,
His Spirit oil glazes me
From the stained wooden fixture
He affixed Himself on
He exclaims, His first words…
It is finished
The beginning of life for me
The express image of God's glory

Only begotten Son
Born in me so that I might live in Him
Deliverer delivered from me
Pushing ungodliness out of me
His Divine counsel is rich and valuable
As a crown of jewels spilled from my
Inmost being
I'm about to deliver
A Savior
Give birth to a legacy
Once bowed low, but the Resurrected
Lifts me so high
I can only perceive my worth by looking
Down on it from above
Where I sit
Shrouded in royal purple
Spiritual heavenly places
Loyal to the Christ who's
Delivered me from all my sins

Salvation of God

The once made offering has been paid for you
Christ's love shed down a piece of old, rugged wood
Poured and flowed from generations ago til now
To ransom your soul
He took thick thorns to His brow
Freed.
Redeemed.
Released from fraud
Your wicked mask faces
The salvation of God
Obeyed in full
Your soul bank secure
Placing trust in the only sacrifice that's pure
Obscured from sight, fright of death no more pulls
The salvation of God strongly removes the wool from our eyes
That disguises the lies
From the father of them and
From his demons inside
Who wishes to hide
In a stumbling Christian's pride,
Dressed in blame-shifting,
Sifting our minds
Smothering spiritual thrashes
Recovering from sackcloth and ashes
Salvation of God
Soothing all of our rashes
Fighting back with the word
Choking back absurdities
That Christ's death long ago buried in me
The fast lane of insanity
Can't handle this vanity
Spitting you're saved

Yet only crippled profanity
Tripled inhumanity
Looking for a cure
Forgetting the resurrection
Brought us back from the lure
And the lust of indignation
The enemy regulating…
Salvation of God
Come quickly
Delegating
More disciples for Him
Searching for fruit purged from the stem
Searching for recruited followers left on the limb
Retrieved from the fall
Delivered from the foe
Tracing the steps left in each tomorrow
The Salvation of God
Not comprehended by man
But given to each one that
Obeys the commands
To stand in line with the shepherd
Stand with the vine
With the Master of all creation
With the maker of all mankind
Endeavoring not to stray
From our lifeline today
Salvation in God should be a very bold taste
To the tongue we're to guard
With the heart we protect
From satan's fiery darts
Learning never to neglect
What's within each being
The spirit of God is not just wind

He grows inside and dispels the blaspheming lie, the deadliest
sin
Crying for peace
Making no room for the Accuser,
The loser of the best
Abuser of the elect
Lord, keep your children loosing themselves in you, in check
Mature in Christ,
Ripening soldiers of might
Turmoil they defeat,
Defenders of everything right
The war on iniquity abated
Children of God awaited security
Because priestly impurity
Warranted a Lamb's purposed surety
Certain his loyalty to death would commit the lost to royalty
for life
Even to temptation He wasn't exempt
Which makes Him a worthy sacrifice
That can never be matched
Satan's luxurious subtleties don't even scratch the surface
Of His uncontrollable divine purpose
The Salvation of God
Cannot be questioned
The Son of man slain, foreknown
And predestined
The once made offering has been paid for you
Christ's love shed down a piece of old, rugged wood
He beckons to those who know Him not yet
Frankly our God is a giver of spiritual blessings access
Delivering promises you'll never forget
Inside of Him you'll experience life
That only He could beget
Saved and victorious

Live free in Him, yes
Anticipating heaven later to possess

A Rock

My my my my my my *my Jesus* is a Rock in a weary land
Yet my foolish hands build my house on the sand
I know I know better, but I don't do no better
So I must be a walking illusion, seeing truth in confusion
Because that Rock won't move unless
I'm the one that chooses to excuse
Myself from my own stability
Swallow the key that gives me security
Because a Rock won't move and knock me off my groove unless
Thrown in the mind like we throw up our hands when
We've had enough
I can't bank on my own strength and then scream I am tough
You see, I hold a Rock in my hand, not one to throw, but on
One to stand
Let me ask you what can you build on a Rock?
Not a gritty sand castle washed away in a wave
Or a toddler's block tower knocked over in rage
Or a popsicle stick fence to keep trespassers away
What have you built on The Rock today?
Build your character on this Rock by being honest and true
To who you say you are and *what* for God you will do
True experiences test our growth stunts or growth spurts
Heaping healing and health as we get over our hurts
Because THIS ROCK won't move unless we do
Won't prove us wrong but lead us through
Because He's an Everlasting, Know-How, I Got This Kind of
God
Don't kick against the pricks dear, but set your feet upon This
Rock
AND STAND. Stand like you've never stood before
Annihilating evil before it treads to your front door

Because an invisible rock won't move unless
An Invincible Rock says to
SO STAND. Stand up ladies like you have some sense
Stop backbiting, lying, and ignoring the facts of this…
The reason why we're even here today
To show that there is a more perfect way… to stand
AND STAND on the principles of honor and service
Let me see you raise your hands if you've heard this
                before
Well if you have then, why sister haven't you moved
Closer to THE ROCK that is dwelling in you?
Because your GOOD name is rather to be chosen than rubies
Stop falling, walking, stumbling around in Christ like you're a
newbie
AND STAND. I SAID. STAND with a humbled heart of love
Because we can't get the ball rolling if it's stuck in your glove
Because MY ROCK won't move you unless
You want Him to do what He promised He would in His
Word that's true
So you better STAND on the discipline that will make your
trembling smooth
STAND on the power, love, and sound mind He placed within
each of you
BUILD up your worth because you're too STRONG to be
WRONG
STOP the generational curses that your families prolong
AND STAND. I SAID. STAND! I SAID!
On a ROCK that won't MOVE unless He chooses TO.
And trust me, HE won't.

Our Father

Our Father in heaven thou art
Which be succinct and distinct in our hearts
We honor your name and give
You the fame
Through the praise we impart and proclaim
And we adore you, faithfully striving
To uphold you and be mellifluously
Sound and true in
Our conversation with you
We end our prayers and shout AMEN
But never our thanksgiving begin
We ask amiss, we ask in greed, but my plea
This day is that we ask indeed, and believe in
Thee, the one true God who should be esteemed
Alpha of our thoughts and Omega of our troubles
The wonderful counselor, of whom there are no doubles
You are the banner when the enemy rages
The peace in our hearts as we go through wearisome
Worrisome, woeful grievous
Stages of our lives
God, you are our God and we
Will ever give you the praise
While your kingdom stays
Thy WILL, not our wills replayed
Yours replays through our minds
Displayed through our actions each and every day for all time
Not just living the way we choose
But walking and working each day for you
We are the tools that YOU use to show this world the truth
Thank you for giving us our daily meds, daily your children
fed
For blessing us with daily news of another soul giving their

lives to You
Forgiving us, of sins long past
For teaching us that lies don't last, but prayers do and
They availeth much and the effects of them many lives you've
touched
And deliverance from tempting trials pleasing our eyes, as we
send
Up timbers of guile
You've blessed us with more than enough while we give
Up appeals and pleas of hatred and lust whining because we
lack that sustaining trust, dealing with unanswered prayers
crushed
But we say lead us not into places that will tempt
As we surround ourselves with the enemy and no armor
Not mentally equipped, looking for deliverance in our pits of
self pity and shame
We forget to pray our Father and forget in Jesus' name
But let us never forget our Father
That we are saved and in our lives dwells the kingdom, glory,
and power
And most of all the joy of You, God Himself

Enough is Enough

I am captive in a sinner's disguise
Looking for grace in satan's smooth lies
Tribulation's greed seems so lifelong
God you're ALL I need, I had it all wrong
I can't get it all together
Yet I am not ashamed
My humility is God's honor
I'm the special child He has named
A perfect woman doesn't need God and
I am so glad that I'm not her
Because I've endured enough tough thorns
This daughter needs her Father
He deliberately bowed low
To deliver grace in my place
When His enough wasn't my enough
I delivered a smack to His face
This immeasurable, misunderstood gift
Grace so foreign, the waiting so tough.
I'm tired of singing this same sad song
Today, I am singing HE is enough.
I speak it like a sales pitch.
Step right up! He's Able! Step right up! He's strong!
But when I'm constantly doing what I Will
I'm only proving what God Won't
I have endured enough tough thorns
Now it's time to speak up
Cause I'm royally adorned in favor
Don't let it pass, I'll drink from that cup
Persecuted, yet still anointed
With a never-ending smile
His enough is my enough
Got me feeling all worthwhile

I may be distressed, but I'm blessed
I'm God's Spirit with Finesse.
I have endured enough tough thorns
I'll add a little more strength to my stress
I have endured enough tough thorns
Praying for their departure yet God says no
Praying for the pain to leave here
God strengthens me and says grow
God's divine influence to move on my behalf
Grace, a sufficient structure with a threefold staff
If God IS Enough
Then Enough is Enough
My falling keeps me humble
While satan's calling my bluff
But He's my desire   My deliverance
My destiny   My divine
My balance of burdens and blessings
Enough's Grace is all Mine
Because His grace will make you smile
When you really want to cry
Because the light is from within
To help you handle thorny times
His powerful rest envelops me
As my purple robe flows down trials road
With a gold-jeweled-toned foot-printed stroll
I'm a picture of His grace retold
I have endured enough tough thorns
I have endured all times too rough
I plead to be released and be reborn
My God's Grace is just Enough

Free Refills

I am empty
I am dry
Yet Lord I try to live for you
You who *restores* my spirit Lord
But I come up short; because I go out and *rejuvenate* me
With greed, bad deeds, jealousy, complacency
And praise you, you who is able to do exceedingly
abundantly;
Above all that I may ever ask or
thank you for not making me like he or she is,
oh God *replenish* me; *refresh* my speech,
Just *refill* my cup, for when my service is parched I can't do
much…
Come in Sunday for a pit stop of pride, falsely *stimulated*,
perpetratingly *revived*
Supplied with my sin, *restocked* on rebuke, God I need a *refill* of
you
I need to be *relieved* and I know you will believe in me to
provide freely, liberally, *renew* me
Please take this envy from me and *bestow* peace in me
Endow me with understanding you instead of underestimating
you
God *invigorate* me with your purpose and love, *revitalize* my
soul, and *reload* my cup
Replace my pain with a newfound elation, Lord strengthen my
heart with a spiritual *donation*
I am empty
I am dry
Yet Lord I try to work for you,
You who *renews* my courage Lord
So that I can be a better servant for you
And worship you in what I know is spirit and truth

So that my head is not bowed low with
Defeat from the blows of satan beating down on me,
But *fortified* from your victory of the fight I've placed in front
of me
Lord I am undone, but know you are with me, to *reinforce* me
Energize me as a zealous soldier in your infantry
God spiritually *animate* me as with sinners I sup; when I
recognize I'm one too please *refill* my cup
Cause I am empty
I am dry
Yet Lord I try to breath for you
You who *revives* the fire Lord, deep in my soul
As I live as I oughta, I'm drinking from the saucer of the
blessings you have *showered* down on me
You have *refilled* me, *rejuvenated* me with the love that I have
only seen in my dreams

Part 7: Relations

Love Like You

God could you teach us how to Love
Like you, Do.
Teach us that if we watch what you do
We can do it too
Show us that waiting will bring us
A love like you… That's true
God we want TO LOVE like You
We know marriage is not to make us happy, but holy
To glorify Him that instituted it, as we ease into it slowly
Show it to the world and continue to thrive
A marriage with sacred wheels is always in stride.
God we want to LOVE like you, Do.
We want to show the world something SPECIAL and TRUE
Stretch ourselves from marriages' physical view
Being spiritually inclined to do it LIKE you
An honest woman wants to submit, respect her husband and
never quit
Showing LOVE like Christ in her words and life; loving LIKE
God is her sacrifice
An honest man will give his life
For His woman and God, as did Christ
He'll cherish this bride of his youth
If he loves himself he'll do it LIKE YOU
Model your marriage after the Christ
The standard of true LOVE
As He gave up His life
With His own precious blood
Husbands love wives as their own body
For no one hates his own flesh
She's presented without spot or wrinkle
He loves his wife as himself
Wives love husbands as they follow Christ

Believe in and trust he'll do what's right
As the head of her family and Christ their head transcends
As the Savior of the union, the two united as friends
You left father and mother and became a spiritual bond
Displayed to the world how the church and Christ are one
God we're learning to Love Like You
Submitting to each other, creating Love that's true
Our Love is become sacred, our hearts bound and new
God's Love in us is better, no other LOVE will outdo
Continue to teach us and mold us how to be like You
Christ's LOVE in our marriages we're about to debut

Possible to Wait

It's possible to think
that because you're single
God understands that your body
Has needs
You know,
that NEED to be met
It's possible to get
All wrapped up in someone
only to have your heart
Beaten and Broken
Cheated and no sense
Can be made of it
Afraid and ashamed
To remain unstained
Celibate you
Sell a bit of your purity
Sell a bit of your mind
Sell a bit of your body
Unchallenged because wisdom can't be found in your eyes
It's possible to look your reflection in the face
And see that stranger
Things have happened than another
Single person questioning God's grace
Foreigner to God's gate, taking the shortcut broad way
to destruction
Popping sex tapes like skittles
Treating worship like riddles
Impossible to understand
That your body's the temple,
Stepping arrogantly through the straight gate
because everyone seems
To have a good thing, but you

Everyone's stepping to wedded bliss
But you
Everyone's made it through broad way
But
True as it may seem
It's possible to believe
You've missed out,
It's a simple thought
So you'd rather
Sell a bit of your time with God
And fraudulently
Create your own sword with jagged edges
Future sketches
Can't craft a masterpiece as well put together and true
As Elohim visionarily
Mapped out His purpose for you
How can you enter in the straight gate
When you're always on the fence,
Always on defense when asked if you'll wait,
You'd rather take the bait, or be it
This is not a game of chase, with your heart on display...
It's possible to save yourself
Even today
Stop looking for love in all the wrong faces
Spaces fill your heart because each lay
Left you even more empty
Spend more time with the Father, not trying to create one
Spend more time as His child, not trying to make one
Enter through the straight gate,
It's narrow, but
Not the broad way
to destruction
It's the narrow road to
Peace of mind

The narrow gate with
instructions for your life
written in blood
Yet others so easily walk through the doors
of your purity
and the spirit leaves
along with your common sense
Now you're living crooked religion
Making rookie provision
For your soul
Daily tempted to mate, but when duty calls
Your mission is wait
And work
Immersing your heart with spiritual freight
Instead of satan's hate to be the only one single in the room
Mentality
Desperately seeking
Flattery is deceitful
Redeem your mind
Of the smooth dating doctrines
Which are supposed to help you find
the One
But are you the One who you are looking for is looking for
Don't get so busy awaiting that call or that text,
So into feeling sex
that you can no longer feel your heart beating
uncontrollably…warning you that, you're losing yourself
he loves me, so I give it up
my convictions
that tell me,
he's really not the one
but she's single and I'm here
so I give it up
your integrity,

You gave it up
your credibility
You give it up
Every time,
wisdom blind
Your sanity maligned
Losing your mind
But you don't have to lose anymore
Don't have to choose uncertainty
Anymore
Don't have to have the blues anymore
Don't have to be confused
Because single doesn't have to mean you're not whole
anymore
You have the whole
Spirit of God dwelling within
You can win against your curiosities
And relational whims
It's possible
To wait
And choose the truth way
The open gate
Place your body under subjection to
The sure place
Fall for His grace
Your mission is to
conquer your craves
And save yourself
A deep, intimate
Fulfilling space
with the Lover of your soul
He didn't hesitate to give up all for you
So, it's possible for you
to wait for Him

I Have a Right

I wanna sing a love song
          about innocence stolen
          about singleness frozen
song about 7 years of celibacy chosen
I have the right to stand UP
I have the right to stand UP and
look you in the face because
I'm okay with the fact, that
It's been 7 years since I've dated
but I'm not ashamed to stand UP
because I have the right to
stand UP
and choose this moment as my life
traveling missionary my guide
I'll go as He sends me
Here. I. Am.
Although
I'm drowning in a bed of fears at night
as I'm running from the former years of life that seemed so
simple
but tonight's good morning is a step outside of a second
and in this minute I have the right to
stand UP
and be me   freely
God that dwells underneath my caramel skin
flowing through my blood cells which is just recycled
salvation in me
salivating for the Word like Pavlov's dogs
hearing a bell that pulls me from the recess of sin into the
school of forgiveness
I'm through playing
I have a right to sing and stand UP

64

I have a right to sing and stand UP
re-tell the story of a little girl without a daddy
who had a mother who brought temporary father figures into
the home
watching them drink with her, or beat her,
she watched her keep them and refuse her sometimes
then mama ran away one night   to grandma's…yeah, I
remember that night
a choice was made.
I could live with mama or enjoy this new house I'd craved
I chose the safest route even though I would have to walk the
longest route to school as
my brothers were bused off to wherever they wanted to go…
I did.
Went away to a safe space… away from afraid
Who gives a little girl a choice?
A little girl with a tiny voice and a pen? I wrote my way out
then
I slept through it with a few, but mainly felt alone. I flirted to
stay afloat. I fought to stay important
It took a village to raise me even though I never really had a
home
It took a village to tell me I would have to learn some things
on my own.
It took a mama teaching me early to cook because she'd be
working double shifts
It took a grandmother making sure I stayed in church even if I
didn't want to
         go, but I did want to go…anywhere but home
It took a village of older sisters telling me that it was okay to
leave because it held no glory for me who'd tell the story of me
anyway?
It took a village showing me that a girl shouldn't have to force
a man to love God

It took a college village to teach me never to settle
It took a village to raise me
It took brothers to change me and the way I thought about family
It took a village of familiarity behind bars so I wouldn't be ashamed of ours
I had no home, but a village that looked out for me
I can turn and thank God for that now.
Because once the Son of man had nowhere to lay his head and feel safe either
I was able to leave that place after years of not finding myself
had my car break down on me, between 7 hours away from
my youth and 5 hours to adult on her own…I felt like
Abraham who wasn't sure what was going on,
          but God
was limiting my sexual mobility
Because 16 years ago, my virginity pilfered, masked as
wanting it because of love unraveling a ravishing desire in me.
A car would have only
          driven me to a future I didn't need to see… at least
that's what I tell myself
Because from sixteen to twenty-three
I was independently de-flowered and shorn
7 years without direction
From twenty-three to thirty I gave it up, gave one away, lost a
lot, but gained me.
7 years of self-reflection
And now I can freely be because
7 COMPLETES ME
At 30,
Those 7 years of singleness gave me the right to stand UP for
myself
The right to stand UP   for myself because I found me
I have a story of overcoming to tell.

I also have a right to keep it to myself,
So, when you get to know me,
If you want to know me,
I have the right to take my seat or
Stand UP and
Fill in the blanks for you

Love Frames

It's time for us to grow up
In Christ
Giving humbly our service
Our sacrifice
Joining hands to reach a concerted
Action
Making God's house a place
Of sinner subtraction
Speaking Love,
Being Love,
Doing Love,
Showing Love
Because
Love surrounds the masterpiece,
Every member fits in the puzzle,
Nothing missing,
Forsaken,
Forgotten,
No thoughts are ever muzzled
Each one respects another's mind
No back talking
Nor sister left behind
All of us women have a place, have a role
Harmonizing us sisters within the whole
Love has the four corners of this frame
Healing…
Obeying…
Protecting…
Enduring…
Together in Jesus' name
Our aged sister becomes the neglected part
And the body of Christ now infected art

Our younger sisters so spiritually fit
But rarely given a chance to represent
An out of place love cannot understand
The needs of the few faithful
Or our Father's dreamland
So we should be mentally in sync
And live
Emotionally rethink
As the whole body cemented together
We speak
And give.
In connected circles, making
Every joint work
Flexible and ready to seek
Our renowned rebirth
And God's Love—
This covers our frames,
From the petite to the bigger
Aims
Effectually working to proclaim the name
Of Christ our reason for having this claim
Love Frames
It candidly speaks
Of my hand fitting in yours
As the devil we defeat
Because we've raised our swords
To others it would seem as
Make-believe
We laugh sisters
Knowing in truth
We were conceived
And the dream has become
Reality now
As each one of us shows

Our spiritual daughters
Just how
Love Frames
It maintains
It sustains
It obtains
It remains
Love…
Frames
Our hearts
Love…
Brings us together
Into the family of victory
The only positive
Repeated history
With the same ending
Unity.

Lip Service

We speak hate gently,
Envy freely, despise feeling
He say, she say mentality beaming
Our righteous outward appearance
Gleaming, while inside scheming
With hypocrisy
This necessary burden of villainy
We must set free and not feed with
Greed, the sound truth you bleed
This hypocrisy—the black sheep of Christianity, is
Driving righteous minds to insanity
Thriving viciously
Spitting spiritual profanity
This antiquated begotten evil has
Pure children full of iniquity
Equally sipping and tripping over beams in each other's eyes
Hypocritical lip service reserves no lies, but
Relinquishes genuine emotions held inside
Humility capsized
Thieves of truth—disheveled and uncouth
Smiling in your face, slithering prudes
Claiming holier than thou,
Profaning the Holiest, now, risen Savior
Are you through…defaming the faithful few—unthankful you
Forecasting hypocritical news of what you got
And who you are to prove, the real Christian your
Lies have subdued. Be renewed in your mind
Promote your potential; abolish your pride.
See you have broken down moral walls
Dismantled conscience sprawled
To revitalize drama through empty words and all
Exalting selves, standing tall, blowing trumpets

And hailing every good you do
Yet blessings you neglect from He who rewards you through
His power, so at this
Hour, you should decide to change, don't wait until it
becomes too late
No more have your mentality lame
Or desensitized and mesmerized by the Father of lies
For you have long lost that game
Woe to you hypocrites, let God calm your
Insecurity, inferiority fits, and run
A race that you can win—woe again because
You're stuck in your ways afraid
To change, blind to potential
Focused on the same, here we go again circumstance
But now will you take a chance
On the life God's given you to advance
And not be stifled with lip service—and unnerve this
unrighteousness
That only keeps you down

Part 8: Identity

Reflections

I'm sick and tired of acting like nothing is wrong
Like every time I look in the mirror I don't start singing this
same old sad song
About why me, and why now, why this and not that, but
never about how God has
Blessed me to even see my reflection in this mirror that I call
my life
And then I skip to the bridge and slow jam to a voice that says
Have you even turned around to thank Him yet?
But while I am so busy looking at myself in the mirror
I AM is wondering have I developed spiritual amnesia
Forgetting how great He is and how good I got it
Taking lightly what has been done for me and mourning
Over my good and precious gifts that come down from above,
Yet He's renewing my life every morning with His love
I must desire slavery over freedom
Because I keep shackling my peace, picking up my cottonous
cantankerous carnality,
and being in bondage to my own bitterness
I must desire slavery over freedom
because I keep serving up my body to the massa
Instead of sacrificing my life for the Master who has released
and redeemed me because
I'm too busy whipping my hair back and forth to realize He's
not even looking at me
like that anyway
All the while eating doubt for dinner, feasting on my leftover
issues of unforgiveness, unworthiness, and unrepentant beans
And beams in my eyes got me tripping over my disguise of
lies, and deceit,
from the enemy

who told me I would never be restored from the sores of abuse,
molestation, and failure
or at least not the way I think I should be.
And while some of us are waiting for a man to relieve us
God is waiting for us to partake of the manna that redeems us
Our Master, Almighty, Nice, Nurturing, Abba that frees us
And brings our minds to the peaceful revelation that all the
mess we're
          hanging on to
was already hung up on the cross for me and you
To live our lives
Free from the stress of sin so we can start stressing Him in our
conversations with others
instead of pressing on and on about why we don't like how
we were freed
Then we smother the fire shut up in our bones because
although He has renewed my heart, restored my spirit, and
redeemed my soul…
I'm just not feeling it.
I go back to my comfortable seat of sin and woe, holding on to
the notion that the commotion satan has caused in my life is
greater than the broken one that saved my life
Yet your lost stuff can be restored,
Your lost self can be renewed,
Your lost soul can be redeemed if you really wanted it to be
So sister what's your reflection looking like?
Are you standing up straight with peace in your hand?
Are you walking in step with your Master's command?
Or are you still complaining about your glass being cracked,
because all you see is your
situation looks whack?
Constantly eyeballing your reflection in the mirror
But have forgotten what manner of woman that lies in ya

Yet, some of us won't understand this truth, so let me say it in
King James Version for you

Sisterern:
Ye mustn't taketh thy life for granteth, Giveth it to thine Father
in heaven and be-eth free.
Free from thine misery. Free from thine agony. And let not
wickedness be named among thee. Don't smiteth thy worth
with worries, killeth thy smile with stubbornness, or beateth
thy body with brokenness. Fret not, my child! Abhor evil and
cling to what is good. The Son of God delivereth thee from thy
foes, so Riseth up from thy bed and walketh renewed; Come
forth in praise and jubilee restored; and See-eth the kingdom
of thy God redeemed…

But until you live the story personally
Receive the Lord purposefully
Know for real that He IS real you'll regretfully continue to
serve the enemy
I'm sick and tired of acting like nothing is wrong
Like every time I look in the mirror I don't start singing the
same old tired song
But today, that must change
I must take my rightful place; being the image of one saved
I must release myself from slavery, reclaim my freedom and
embrace some bravery
Head to the north with my eyes fixed on Christ
Not so busy staring in the mirror, that I don't notice what's not
right
BECAUSE God REDEEMED – recovered ownership of your
sin-sick soul
AND, God RESTORED – putting together what was broken
and torn

YES, God RENEWED – returning your body to its original functioning form
So, take off the shackles and begin to live free
Noticing the reflection of Christ dwelling in thee
I said take off the shackles and begin to live free
Noticing the reflection of Christ looking right back at thee

Dressing the Spirit

I'm IN secure
SEE CURE
Was the diagnosis that He gave me when He birthed me with
AHHH
The breath of life
God, my fortress, my rock,
My sustainer IN strife
But somewhere along the line I forgot about Christ
Saying He would leave me another Comforter.
The same spirit I've forsaken
Left to die. Soul naked and
Shaking like a felon getting ready to lie
But, I, I can handle the truth
That what I'm about to say will scold these skinny thighs
Molded and folded these jeans so many times
My stomach hurts
Squeezing into denim
Quenched spirit burst
Wide open-
Ended questions like:
Does this shirt make me look fat?
Is my hair okay?
Should I have worn it straight with the kinks out the way?
Do these shoes scream that I'm poor?
Am I finally that beauty queen someone's been searching for?
Or not?
I must be trying too hard
To be what the world calls hot
Found out mama didn't raise no fool
But mama humbly begot
A fashion DON'T:
Don't blend IN, Don't pretend

Don't realize my beauty shines from within
Don't match-less grace cover the girl IN me
Don't underestimate the spiritual Essence, you see
On the front page perpetrating like Job
Who questions God while skimming through Vogue
Gathering up treasures down here a must,
While the spirit INside sewed up, worn out rusts
Exposing our spirit to what not to wear
Not peace
Not gentleness
Not quietness
Unaware
That the church is getting praise confused with paparazzi
And each camera shot knocks me
One notch closer to the edge of the lens
Captures the 20/20 pounds I've put on instead of the 20/20
equals 40 rounds of prayers I count on
To make me like a bird so I can fly far far away
Only to be shot back down by my own mistakes
Don't notice that our daughters out here are trying to be
grown
And mamas acting crazy, looking for their own
Identities IN miniskirts and slimming slacks
Supposed to preparing for a mansion, while your spirit is
living IN a shack
Honey, this world is not your home
So stop building up your earthly house with layaway jewelry
and clothes on credit
You'll find yourself IN debt, regretting
Each cuff that shackled your spirit
Dressed IN the finest, yet
Spirit denied His shine
Decked out like royal
But to your own soul disloyal

Peeping for outfits IN your closet
Versus praying for others adding sweet spirit deposits…to your life
Queen   of the people watcher
Talking about every atrocity you see, but can't confess your need to be
Someone other than yourself
How do you look?
Shook like a caught pickpocket crook
Stealing pieces of your own joy
Did you forget godly doesn't go out of style?
As soon as Eve put on those leaves she changed
Hiding from God, dressed IN shame
Covered with leaves left her still afraid
As He called out to her, He still calls out today
But we're too busy calling each other out,
When our phone is the one ringing,
Satan getting clingy sending hate messages to your spirit
That's so full that God's word can't get IN.
Damagin' who we are IN Christ,
Focusing on the latest trend,
Than the fated sacrifice of Jesus, our friend.
We by-pass each other because we've "dressed" the part
Ignoring the scars of ugliness,
Unworthiness,
Undeservedness, that satan has placed on our hearts.
How many smudge secrets have disguised you,
Grudges kept, numbered behind you, love relationships you have, besides you & satan?
Rise up now alive and claiming your breakthrough
Because every tattoo ain't ink
You can rethink the way you've dressed you
You can laser remove your hurts with a truth
Shout of renewal and insert permanently

The things, which God has prepared for you,
The deep things of God which look through you,
That thin layer of façade that the world sees as you,
Don't just pray for another's purity that God can't even see IN
you
Suffocating your spirit because you
Can't be self-controlled or trusted to be you
Soul on parole, but never free from your abuse
Your flesh wants what it is used to; I get it;
Wants to keep you in bondage to the enemy's view of beauty,
Forgetting
That what's IN you, is what will last
That what's IN you determines if your past,
Will bind you or release you
To glorify God with class
Because confidence is attractive when accompanied with
praise
Quietness is beautiful, when it's peaceably with grace
Your spirit is decked out when
Gentleness permeates
From the way you sit at the Master's feet in wonder
Looking IN the Word
Not looking for a number to define your worth
So, my sisters be secured
SEE CURED is the diagnosis
That He gave you when HE blessed you with life
You can serve with a strut because you're
Serving IN Christ
What God sees IN you matters
What He notices is from withIN
That spirit of yours catches His eye,
Oh, those scars, He shatters them
So give yourself away
There's no reason to feel grim

To Him you're beautiful always
Always beautiful INside to Him

82

Undying Flock

I am not who you think I am
Shut up in a portal blessed
A vacillating, immortal mes…sage waiting to be proclaimed
I'm stepping high in heels,
But creeping low in worth, ashamed
A grown woman standing on
Tippy toes to find herself
A seed of the undying flock
Spirit tick-tocking like a Timex clock
Hailing from the tribe of inexterminating beauty
I'm not a size skinny anymore, so sue me
My walk is a pure, undeniable strut
Clothed in the finest with a big old…
But what really matters is my size inside
Am I puny in spirit or gigantic in pride?
If I believe His words then I cannot die,
Because well, my Father in heaven, He cannot lie
So I stand rooted in unceasing favor,
Blessed and crowned, my eternal flavor
Grounded and abounding
My kinswomen surround me
I'm imperishable
Yet why do I feel deplorable?
Yes, my Father named me and
Counted each strand in me,
But the enemy man-handled and
Laced my indestructible frame with gold chains
Now, I'm primping like I came from Jared's
Limping into the background,
Incorruptible, despicable me
Not recognizing that while I'm so busy stepping into your gift
Mine perisheth

Skimpy and wondering why my territory hasn't expanded yet
Past the age of understanding that
My worth doesn't lie in riches
I'm imperishable, but too big for my britches
I'm an everlasting seed
Permanently praising me,
With ingrown untruth roots
Sprouting from every extremity
Forgetting Thee's
Supposed to be supplying me with infinite humility
Will He ever?
See that my heart is dwindling
Well, I never!
Pray.
Never stay on fire for Christ
Forever straying from my sacrificed
Ticket to freedom
Continually repenting for the hidden woman of the heart
Is starting to get on my nerves
While my Lord's imploring for the forgiveness He's preserved
You see
Although I put on Christ in baptism,
I can't look past this invisible prism
Of imperishablism
Should be feeling like the new self,
But I'm perishing looking forward to being somebody
else…other than me
I'm not that holy and beloved,
Whole armor of God sporting
Righteous, merciful, compassionate waving
My fist at God because I don't feel I'm worth saving
Permitting kindness to the first man that humiliates me
I'm the first to let strength gently pass from me
But God.

God put His laws in my heart
God.
God put His words in my mouth
God cloaked me in Spirit
Put my negative mind in timeout
Dissected my worth
Implanted purity in me
Operated patiently
With incorruptible and eternity His surgical instruments
Cutting off my sinful
Childish things
Slicing the lustful eye in me
Angry me, bitterly
Putting off sex for intimacy—
Putting off complaints and complacency—
Putting off pride and jealousy—
My old man starving
Yet, spirit starts rejoicing
in me
Undressing the flesh
With an unending prayer to be refreshed
And renewed
I'm an imperishable princess
Clothed in deity, behooved
To speak only of His good pleasure
Measuring His grace instead of my waist
Worshipfully plump and rotund with
Appreciative juicy praise lips to Almighty God
I'm a sheep of the undying flock
Building my lifelong inheritance on
The Rock
The righteousness of Christ secures my soul
Regenerated daily by the Holy Ghost
Whom I denied, more than once upon a time

Because 'tis better to surrender my life today
Than deal with the tragedy of my broken state
For so long I've tried to prolong my life
Only managing to create a disaster
But I will stand up tall
With my baggage and all and
Give it over to the Master
Because He is everything to me, to me
He is everlasting and everything I need
He is undeniably, unbelievable
Unthinkable, unsinkable
He is Love unbeatable
Imperishable Adonai, Lord Master
Placed within me Eternal life
He is unmistakably the Lord who heals – Jehovah Rapha, my
God He will
Enliven me with a love so deep
A spirit so free
I'll be endlessly leaving provision footsteps (for my seed)
With my every degree of joyfulness
Everyday YOUR name I'll bless
For creating me - Perfectly
The God-3 molded and sculpted US just right
So we - must show up with our hands outstretched in
surrender to Him
Not so concerned with the mess of this world that keeps us
forever dying in our sins
You, sister, are an undying flock,
spirit tick-tocking like a Timex clock, building your
inheritance on the Rock…
You are destined to win

Wilt Thou Be Made Whole

"It's about time I got up from here"
Say the wounds on my soul
I'm tired of wearing this Band-Aid
Wardrobe
It ain't cute
Buttoning up the years of hurt that never heal
Zipping up tight the lips that spill
Hate speech to me
Every year
New resolutions for the same old problem
No change and I'm still broke.
Doctor?
My soul is sick
And I can't seem to get well
Scrapes and scars war
Against me and I'm
Bandaged in guilt's hell
Dragging my baggage like loads of dirty clothes
Is there a Doctor in this house?
Because I want to be made whole
Fearing the distance to wellness
Complete wholeness
Got me back pedaling
Selling my soul to this sin again
Wasting away and spinning in my
Setbacks
Spending all my greenbacks on
Dr. Seuss, yet hadn't learned my lesson
Dr. Oz still hadn't prescribed the curing medicine
Dr. Miracle's got me going in circles,
Sitting session after session with Dr. Phil, and I still can't get
my mind right

I've got issues
Is there a REAL Doctor in THIS house?
Who from these chains can cut me loose?
I'm willing to get down to meet Him
Are you?
I'm unclean but unashamed with a
Blood problem that has Jesus' name on it
So let me take this step towards Him
Oooo, but I want to touch that!
Try this!
And get next to everyone else,
But the Prince of Peace
What are you reaching for in your loneliness?
Your Only-ness
Only one without a job,
Only one without a man,
Only one without a healing,
Only one without a plan
Now your heart is crying,
A broken mess
You feel like a pile of pitifulness
Inside a pain flows through your veins
You've been speaking this same shame
For years
Growing comfortable instead of growing up
You've been speaking in circles, cheering on
The blame like it invests in you
Woman, God is BEST for you
It's about time for you to
Get up from here and get whole
Get to stepping out of cemented sin
The unforgiving message that grins
In your face
Get to stepping out of demented worth

The forgiveness begins when you reveal your hurts
I tried everything, now I'm trying HIM
I'm hooked on Yahweh
And I'm not turning again
Because His phonics got me speaking
Holy Ghost isms
That sound like
I'm going Solo[w]
I'm So Low
I'm touching Him
I'm So Low
I praise in bass
I'm So Low
My worship looks like push-ups
Forsaking the people who will only step on me
Forsaking the broken story that once claimed me,
Taken advantage of no more,
My Record label is Victory
My Producer is God
I'd rather crawl towards a healing
Than stand with the villains
Of yesterday, long ago, and way back when
No friends, yet I'm still surrounded by a company of angels
No sister can pray hard enough
To get me untangled from Jesus
I want Him.
So bad
I want to be made whole
So I reach forward with hope in my hand
And
Freedom in my step
I'll lunge towards Him
Like that's all in me that I have
Left

Do *you* want Him enough to move?
Do *you* want to
Stop the Groove
of chains digging in your membrane
that had you too insane to choose
Wholeness
       Is a Savior portrayed
Pity party turned into a Favor parade
Wholeness
       Dried up years of your tears
       And made you a daughter
Wholeness
       Deduced your enemies to dust
Because it might look like I'm falling
But I'm fighting
You may think I'm tripping
But I'm skipping for Him
It may seem like I'm crawling
But I'm still standing
Wholly praying to the Almighty
And this Giver of everlasting healing
Isn't the Doctor in this house!
Get up from here and get whole
NOW
Because
12 years didn't keep our sister from the Lord
So what's your problem?
Lay it at the cross
Stop laying down and making your
Body the boss
Go So Low and reach
And then you'll see
That sometimes you'll have to
Walk alone in order to

Walk With Thee
Wilt thou be made whole?
Will you trust in Him?
What are you waiting for?
The Doctor is in THIS House
Ready to heal you, His child

Resurrected Life

If the power to rise lies within us
Why are we still playing dead?
Playing as if we're dead to sin
Spiritually squatting
Claiming
We're living in Him
But refusing to put in the work
Too deep in the grave to see our worth
Too deep in our hurt
To reverse
The pains of our pasts with praise
We've been released, but we're
Too afraid to step out on sin
Too deep
To see beyond our strife
Professing the Resurrected Life, but
Too deep in our complacent comforts
Too deep to call out false doctrine when we commune in our
sacred cliques
Too deep in our Christian conveniences to change
Chain gang chanting and
Remixing songs of Zion
With no hook
Putting in hard labor for the crook,
Who framed us
Too ashamed to
Claim victory in the One who raised us
Who named us?
Because our adoption feels like a pity party
Rather than a praise fest
So we house our spirits in prisons
Laced with velvet and silk

As if bondage is the Luxe life
As if stronghold is a ten-letter word for comfort
As if jail is synonymous to joy
But we've been released from our
Hell cells
Calling on the Lord for who He is
Calling out the devil for what he's not
This Resurrected Life is calling
Calling for a prison break
Calling for a breakthrough
Break through your suffering
Break through your chit chattering
Break through the curses and worthlessness
Break ground and breakthrough to resurrection
And if we've been raised then we need to stand
Stand on His promises
No longer locked up
But yoked up with the Master
Stocked up on living water
Praising His name with lifted hands
A hallelujah outbreak and the church says, *Amen*!
But we should be tired of playing church
Where we go to be
Amused with a weekly dose of
Religious vegetarianism,
Abused with politically charged sermonettes, and
Pumped up with business meeting jargonism
God's elect –
Choosing satan
A malnourished mess searching for a Master
In an abandoned household
There's no meat in our message
More gluten than grace

The only fasting we do is to see how fast we can jump from
our pews and out the door!
I mean we only meet to fashion show
Who can cover up their sins the best
Versus confessing I am covered in I AM
I am… tired of playing church
It's time to be it,
The beloved bride
Who RISES to the occasion
Adorned in her greatness
Mind so tired of counterfeit praise it
Looks like she's sleepwalking
Sweet-talking
The Holy Spirit to release me from my
Wrongs
And then we give the
Enemy a foothold
And he hugs us with a
Stronghold
Once again
We've been deceived to believe
We're too free
So we go BACK to the comforts of bondage
BACK bloodied because we were slaves to sin
Whipping our own bodies into shape
Shaping our hurts into wheels that drive
Us insane
Shaping our minds to receive the lie that
We're never enough
Too Deep
Down
We starve our souls
Living in new age slave quarters
Begging the Master for a

Piece of bread
The same Master who fed over 5000
With a catfish sandwich
A Resurrected Life is
Unashamed to reveal that our history
Was fixed on Calvary
So there's no need to mimic the misery
He felt on the cross
Raised and Upturned
Not turned up
Outstretched and released
Approaching higher ground like Lazarus
Stink clothes and all
But FREE.
Regaining strength one step
At a Time
But I'm stepping in the name of
Love
Because Love Lifted Me
Yet some
Gentile eyes
Have to see resurrection to believe
The war in our members is
Trying to keep us dead
But the SAME power that raised Jesus
From the grave
Is the SAME power we have to be lifted
From the shame
Shouting like Jeremiah who had a fire
Shut up in his bones,
Leaping out of our seats, but not going
Out of our minds
Jumping for joy because
Can't nobody hold me down

Oh no…I got to keep on moving
You're a rephrased scorner into saint
Take up your gravestone
Rise up and walk
Walk by faith not by sight
Walk worthy of the vocation wherewith
He has called you
Walk in the Spirit
Walk on water
Just rise UP you are FREE
To walk in heavenly places with THEE
Great Redeemer of your soul
Resurrected you look down on your life
From above
No longer dirt,
Spirit of blood lifted
Gifted, and released
Filled with eternal wisdom
Covered in I AM

Part 9: Communion

Soul Connection

I want to connect deeply
Be worship fully into Thee
Soul twisted like pretzels
Interlapping praise and
Overlocking blessing with He
Most High
I'm choking with intimacy
With my spirit inside
Swapping deep things
Like mysteries
and histories
of how we communicated before You created me
And
Erected me to sit in
Positional loftiness
Precisionally lost my flesh
Provisionally bought my debt
On the cross
I can't help but get low for You
Adore You
Prostrate and humbled before You
I once stumblingly ignored You
Hurriedly turning to You from sin
I bend
Waist first
Bow face down and honor You
Kneeling as though I fell for You
I pledge my life to You
Encasing my soul into a silent Love language that only You
and I speak
Meditating on Your air… I breathe

Anguish turned to anxiously awaiting a sweet word to make
my heart skip
Bounds
Slip inside or around You
I try to squeeze all that You are into all that I'm not without
You
Master, I need You like a flower reaches up for sun
Like a seed cries out for water
I crave to grow in You
As Your Spirit teaches me all there is to know about You
Your power mesmerizes me
Your mercy captivates me
Grace so fluid it wraps itself in me as if we were conjoined
twins
I want to connect deeply
See clearly Thee
Almighty free me to crack this shell that tries to hide me from
You
This box that demands to darken my view
I burst forth by Your command
I kiss Your hand and swallow Your plans like grapes
And yield up purpose for You
My life a daily sacrifice and love letter
To You
As I offer me
All of me collectedly
Vulnerably I expose myself
And You. Still. Love. Me.
I beg of You
Fill this temple with a dose of a heart that desires only to
please You
I'm drowning in Your love
And my soul still thirsts for You
Oh God, You are my God

I seek for You as soon as I wake up
You overflow my cup with joy
When my soul longs for You, You are near
When my heart cries out for Your love, You are there
To share that Your heart cries for me too
Without You, I sink
I think, no I know, Your heart may even break for me
I love the way we commune
I taste and see that You are good always
You fill me
Blood-connecting spirit leads me
Feeds my hunger for serving thee
You see me
You get me
Therefore, I will praise You with my everything
You are awesomely real and amazingly mine
I lay myself before You
Your name is my comfort
I'm worship fully into You
I rejoice over You with singing
I long to hear You say You love me
You deserve more than
The highest praise
As my days go by
I recount blessings of how I
Can't get enough of You
My soul keeps falling in love with You
I wanna get next to You
So I seek, deeply
Connecting my malignant spirit
To Your super majesty
Freshening mercy
That's lavished upon me
Interlocking praise with overlapping blessings

You make me feel like a
real woman
of God
who lives only to
chase after Your heart
Forever

Fall for Him

You may think I'm tripping, but I meant to fall
I fell at His feet
And begged for wholeness
As if my life depended on it
It did.
Falling Unashamed, I lay
There, prostrate before Him
Wound up my wounds in
Willing worship and
Waited while He welcomed my
Weeping and wiped away my weary
I fell. For Him
I fearlessly leapt forward
Not hearing the crowd that looked down on me
for my daring devotion to
Have the audacity to touch their King
With my unclean hands
I grasped the air in front of me that felt thick as
Smog   thick
Like the lump in my throat
And touched His hem; I tremble, yet approach as
His queen
As if mentored by Esther herself
On how to approach the king's scepter with grace
And even though because of me,
Virtue was taken from Him
He gave me permission to speak
His praises
So I did…
Fell straight to my knees
And spoke
As if my tongue had been singed with a hot coal

I spoke; as one who speaks the very oracles of God
His testimonies
Fall
From my lips
Like subjects kissing verbs
Like vowels needing words to be
Real
Master, my Messiah, I desire to draw deeper into
Thee, follow you wherever you lead
I fall for you with all of me
My plea, a beseeching request to be free
Suddenly He turns to face me
Silently voicing His praises
He rephrases my dirt for Daughter in the midst
of my misfortunate life.
Many of us have been running
In the wrong direction for restoration
For soul calibration
Too out of breath to praise
Too cute to raise our hands in
Worship
Past the finish line of degradation
Falling deep
In desperation for the next man to fill us
His socio-political devastation
Billing us
Every time we sell out the Savior
We say we're thirsty and craving for the
Cornerstone
Chasing after Christ
Yet
Standing too tall in stubbornness
With half-hearted broken spirits
Too fatigued in our pursuits to connect entirely

Sprinting towards a destination, which only
dead-ends to sin
We grimace at grace,
But at lust we grin
Disconnected from our divine lineage
Running away versus towards Him
But it's time to
Shamelessly submit even when the crowds
surround
Even when the people of God doubt
That someone like you could ever be healed
Unscripturally stoned for not
Blending in with those, who speak against Him
I'll fall for Jesus
Before following greed and
risk approaching the Great Redeemer.
It's time to fall face forward into favor
So that obedience leads to
Overblessing
Consuming miracles at daybreak
Falling frozen in faithfulness
The fire in my soul melts me
Like icicles at the cusp of spring
Falling
Into His arms
Come boldly now
Unto your King…
Falling for Him,
Not tripping,
Intentionally reaching up for redemption
For He owns the very thing you may lose for
Loving Him…everything
Anointingly abounding in blessings
Falling from heaven

Unto your being
Astounded
That all is yours
When it's all in His hands
So fall
Unconsciously supine at his throne
Fall
Planking,
Your new posture in his presence
Falling
For Him
So very   unashamed
You empty yourself of you,
So that He can make you whole

Acknowledgements

Poems in this collection have been spoken at various ladies empowerment conferences and other community events. Some have been published in Ladies Lectureship Retreat program booklets, Tracing the Infinite Compilation: The International Library of Poetry, Beneath the Baobab Tree, and the Literary Anthology: Freed-Hardeman University.

Special Thanks

Many thanks to my hometown literary family, The Griot Collective of Jackson, Tennessee who published some of my first poems in *Beneath the Baobab Tree* (Volume II and III); thank you for encouraging me to see my potential as a young poet.

Thank you Shanita, the best friend I have in the world; my sister in spirit, who challenged me to write this book, giving me an unmovable deadline to complete it in our year of daring greatly because you believed Psalm 71:21 *"Thou shalt increase my greatness, and comfort me on every side."* If I could ask God for anything, it's to never lose you! Thank you for your friendship, patience, guidance, love, and support.

Many thanks to my family, who believed in me since I was child; many times silent with their encouragement, yet urging with their lives that I could conquer any dream by fulfilling it.

I have not walked this journey alone. Where could I begin to thank all of those whom have joined me, communed with me, listened to me, walked beside me, taught me, supported me, and urged me to write this book? These poems would not have been possible without the collaboration, encouragement, inspiration, love, and friendship of many women and men of whom I'm eternally grateful.

About the Author

No stranger to motivational prose, Melanie Joyce Johnson is a passionate writer and poet, who specializes in spiritual, poetic, and inspirational writing. She writes, not because she has to, but because she loves to and believes God has called her into this purpose.

Co-founder of Sisters With A Purpose (S.W.A.P.) Ministries, Melanie's varied background in spirituality, psychology, and counseling have provided the perfect foundation for expounding on women's issues in the church where she is highly sought out to present her self-expression poetry pieces at various ladies events. She is co-author of the 9-week devotional book, *It's Over: Finding Freedom By Breaking Negative Strongholds*. She is in development of her own Spiritual Expressive Arts therapy and teaching tool to address the issue of domestic abuse in the church.

Melanie believes in being sensitive to and following the Holy Spirit's leading in all things. Her personal vision is to utilize her creativity and spiritual support skills to bring harmony to the world and bring connectivity back to God. Her favorite scripture is Philippians 4:6-7, *"Be careful for nothing; but in everything by prayer and supplication with thanksgiving let your requests be made known unto God and the peace of God, which passeth all understanding, shall keep your hearts and minds through Christ Jesus."*